COLLATERAL *Damage*

By QuiNina Sinceno

Grief is life's collateral damage, but its purpose is not to damage us permanently.

Collateral Damage

Copyright © 2022 by QuiNina Sinceno

GDI Enterprises, LLC

All Scripture quotations, unless otherwise indicated, are taken from the Holy Bible New King James Version. Other versions quoted are Message and King James Version. All rights reserved.

All rights reserved. No part of this publication may be reproduced, stored in a retrieval system, or transmitted in any form or by any means-electronic, mechanical, photocopy, recording, or any other e for brief quotations in printed reviews, with the prior permission of the publisher.

Printed in the United States of America

Author: QuiNina Sinceno

ISBN: 9781737708766

I dedicate this book to the hearts who have experienced loss and have yet to heal. May your pain be soothed through the words of this book.

In loving memory of Jane E. Sinceno, Henry S. Winfrey Sr., Warren Sinceno Sr., Melvin Jenkins, and Tamika Tate Clerk.

Contents

Preface

15 | Elephant in the Room

25 | Soul Pains

43 | But Why God?

57 | Dark Days

73 | Collateral Damage

83 | Heavy Lifter

Preface

Grief is life's collateral damage, but its purpose is not to damage us permanently. When I heard these words, I was in the middle of dealing with grief. I was hurting, disappointed, and even had the nerve to be angry with God. I'm sure you can imagine my response to it. It was not exactly a phrase to rejoice about initially. It was one of those sayings that are hard to swallow; in my community, we call them "hard sayings". The truth hurts sometimes but the purpose of truth is not to cause damage but to provide freedom.

And You shall know the truth and the truth shall make you free."
John 8:32

This Means the truth will develop you, it will shape you, and it will also destroy the effects of bondage that believed lies can place on your mind and heart.

When Collateral Damage was placed on my heart, I was in search of relief for the pain that ached in my heart and for the hearts across the world who were experiencing loss after loss after loss. During my prayer times, I would weep bitterly as I prayed for those who were losing their loved ones, their faith, jobs, homes, relationships, and ways of living that they once knew. I cannot honestly say I have nor have had any desire to be acquainted with grief, however, we have seemed to cross paths on more occasions than I'd prefer. Usually, when we as authors begin to write on a particular topic, we have deemed ourselves to be the experts of such and feel we have much to offer on the subject as a Master of Information. I'm not quite sure if anyone would volunteer to become familiar with grief in such a way that one becomes an expert because with expertise there is a level of experience that is required and expected. The true nature of an expert can function in any arena because one can maximize any level of experience by absorbing the hidden treasures of any subject and articulating them to others effectively. So, though grief and I are not friends I've learned quite a bit from having to experience many losses. This is merely an attempt to articulate the wisdom gained through my encounters. Thus, Collateral Damage was written to heal the epidemic of grief that this world is experiencing in hopes of bringing nations together. We are all experiencing the same pains from loss, but only a few of us are crazy enough to publicly open pandora's box.

It is almost as though this book has a spiritual horror story type of feel. We spend so much time avoiding dealing with grief that it is quite frightening. Part of me believes it could be one of the reasons there is an alarming rise in mental instability. This subject is definitely not easy. Believe me, I understand this will be an uncomfortable journey, but it will bring healing as well.

Sometimes healing begins at simply knowing you are not alone. So, as you continue reading, you will meet others like yourself who involuntarily became acquainted with grief: Job, David,

Rizpah, Naomi, and Jesus Christ. We will be examining their griefs and responses to find encouragement and answers as to how to handle our own.

Opening our perspectives to adjust through the focus of new lenses will aid in coping with trauma. For those of us who have experienced trauma, we know trauma can be so isolating and silencing at times. Especially during the moments when those around us cannot relate and find themselves muted without words to say. We often hurt more as we notice their silence becoming louder as their distance broadens. In their defense, the silence may only be an inability to articulate not knowing what to say or how to comfort you. And you have no clue how to tell them what you need. Isolation makes its move as your trauma creates a wedge that grows with your grief. It would be nearly impossible to avoid feeling alone. However, my friends will prove that you are not alone and that there is a Balm in Gilead.

Elephant in the Room

Introduction

By now I'm sure you have walked into a room and felt as though something was going on in the room that no one wanted to or dared talk about. But the unspoken remained just as present as the individuals present. The older folks would sometimes say, "you can cut the tension with a knife", as though tension was a physical object. It's true, feelings and emotions can sometimes be so strong their energy creates a sense of a personified presence in a room. Yet there are times when those feelings, though obvious, are ignored because it makes us confront such strong emotions face to face. Since emotions are originated in one's heart, I would say confronting one's state of heart can be quite a challenge for most of us if not all of us depending on how deep into our hearts we must travel to reach the root of the displayed emotion.

> **Taboo**
>
> socially prohibiting discussion or association of a person place or thing

Do you remember? You could sense there was something that needed to be addressed but was intentionally avoided. Such awkwardness. Whether the opted silence was a result of not wanting to ruffle feathers of anger or not wanting to ignite pain. The elephant in the room remained evident as taboo staked its claim.

Depending upon the type of culture you were born into there are quite a few different approaches to dealing with topics that may be taboo to others. Ignoring the elephant in the room is not always the best idea because avoiding and deflecting as an attempt to ignore what makes one uncomfortable only prolongs the inevitable. At some point, one must deal with the elephant because it is occupying space that has crowded the atmosphere.

There is an elephant in the room of every country in the world. No one seems to want to talk about it, so we have chosen to continue in our pain. If we are all honest, we have a commonality that every race and ethnicity has had to continue to stand in a room with as though it does not exist. Our elephant is the pain of grief that we as a world have all had to live with daily during this era. Continuing to turn a blind eye toward the silent cries will not make the pain go away.

> **Grief**
>
> sorrow, an overwhelming emotion caused by experiencing loss, often a result of someone's death

Grief is unlike us. We classify ourselves as superior to others based on the labels we give them. Grief has no prejudice towards what we have prejudices towards. Country, race, ethnicity, creed, religion, political party, community, financial and social status, language, educational level, or the lack thereof are all irrelevant qualifications to avoiding grief.

Naturally, we are prone to only think of grief as the emotional state that is the result of experiencing the loss of another human. However, I've come to learn grief to be more than the loss of another person, but it can also be a result of experiencing loss in general. I believe that one can grieve anything that was held as a treasure. A patient who newly discovered terminal cancer can grieve what was once their perfect health. A providing husband can grieve a career that once gave stability to his family as he tells his wife they have lost their home and will have to move with no place to go, just as she can grieve the safety she once felt in her home. A mother may grieve the relationship she once had with a child who has decided to reject their upbringing of Christian morals and dignity, causing their relationship to become estranged.

Grief has many faces and comes in many shapes, sizes, and forms but at its core is a triggered emotion that is overwhelming and burdensome. It is hard to talk about, hard to think about, hard to be in a room with. Like an elephant, it takes up massive amounts of space in our lives upon arrival filling the rooms of our hearts with pain and sorrow. And just like fully grown elephants, the weight of grief can be very heavy. The good news is, though elephants are heavy they are still moveable objects.

Sometimes the size of a thing can look to be impossible to move. But according to physics, what seems impossible for a lesser object like yourself to lift is possible through leverage and friction reduction. In physics leverage always requires an amount of force when lifting a load. Friction reduction requires a type of lubricant or oil. In our case, we will be relying on oil. Friction reduction may be challenging and uncomfortable but remember it is the anointing that destroys the yoke and every ounce of oil produced is proceeded by a moment of crushing.

I encourage you to embrace your healing process, realizing that unattended wounds almost always become infected. Consider the next few chapters as wound care. The necessary discomfort. It may take us until the end of the book to get the right leverage, but I believe grief will be lifted and replaced by the yoke of Jesus Christ.

For my yoke is easy, and My burden is light.

Matthew 11:30

Soul Pains

Naomi

May I introduce to you, a woman of great strength and wisdom? She suffered quite a bit of loss in the form of material things as well as loved ones. Her pain as a wife and mother placed many tears on her cheeks. Her story is one worth noting. Most times her story is told as a prelude to her daughter-in-law's story as the main event. However, today Naomi is the star. Here's Her Story.

Naomi married Elimelech and bore two sons, Mahlon and Chilion. They were originally from Beth-lehem-judah but moved to Moab because of a famine. While in Moab her husband dies and a bit over ten years later her two sons die, leaving behind their wives Orpah and Ruth. Later, Naomi heard that there was bread back home and decided to take the journey. Ruth has invited herself on the trip, ignoring all of Naomi's attempts to send her back to Moab. Naomi was adamantly attempting to isolate herself because she was still grieving and bitter. So bitter that when she returned home, she told them to call her Mara for she felt God had dealt bitterly with her. But God continued to provide, and Naomi continued to tolerate her new daughter.

As she started to warm up to her presence, they developed a stronger relationship. She even counseled her on how to acquire the attention of a potential husband who was her relative. We no longer read of her being called Mara, but instead, end her story with her praising God amongst the women of her community as they praised the Lord with her. God restored her joy.

Then the women said to Naomi, "Blessed be the Lord, who has not left you this day without a close relative; and may his name be famous in Israel! And may he be to you a restorer of life and a nourisher of your old age; for your daughter-in-law, who loves you, who is better to you than seven sons, has borne him." Then

Naomi took the child and laid him on her bosom and became a nurse to him.

Ruth 4:14-16

As you've read Naomi went through quite a bit. Any route she would have chosen would have been a route that most could not argue with considering her pain and sorrow. Yet, even in that, she chose what she chose, I'd like to understand why one day, but for now let's just dissect what she did.

Some Noami would agree that a change of environment was a natural response and others would disagree by feeling leaving Moab would have been leaving her family. I'd like to ask you. Why should Naomi have stayed in a strange land after the death of her husband and sons? I believe the answer to that question would be the answer to moving on versus moving forward.

Moving Forward to Move On

Contrasting two ideologies that are so closely related may cause controversy, but I'd ask that you focus on the principle of what I'm about to say rather than the wordplay. It is possible to move forward without moving on.

> It is possible to move forward without moving on.

The reason I say that is because Naomi decided to leave Moab, the barren place of her sorrow, to head to Judah, the place of praise but she brought her bitterness with her. She made steps towards a place of fruitfulness and potential growth but brought baggage with her. So often we try to move forward, continue to go to work, we try to do things that appear as though we are ok and are normalizing our lives, but the whole time we're carrying the baggage of grief with us. We pack our bitterness from feeling left alone and abandoned, guilt from not being there as we should have been, anger with God, and resentment towards others. She picked up her pain even though she had to carry it with her. She could have chosen to stay in Moab to die just as her family had, she could have chosen to be buried next to her husband and children. Naomi was beyond childbearing years, her sons were both old enough to have wives, so it's safe to say she was already on the latter end of her life. She could have chosen to die the way they had, but she didn't. She decided she wasn't going to die the way her family had. She decided to put action towards moving forward.

Moving forward is not always as difficult as moving on for those who can easily compartmentalize their lives. Taking the first steps in moving forward can sometimes be one of the hardest things to do because of our entangling emotions. Our perspectives play a huge role in both. Moving on to some is seen as letting go. It implies an underlying dismissal of that which is left behind. I'd say Naomi did no such thing and personally believe it is unreasonably ridiculous to expect anyone to forget or dismiss who/what they love as though it/they never existed. Might I suggest a different perspective? Moving on is not forgetting or dismissing, it is an acknowledgment of what was to make you better for what is to come. A continuation of a reason to continue. Naomi's moment of moving on was when she embraced what was left in honor of what was gone. When she embraced the new baby with joy and a grateful heart with a desire to continue her family's legacy is when we can truly say she moved on. She embraced a new "why" for living, which honored her family and those who were no longer with her.

Moving on looks more like taking those intimate moments and plans that you may have had and finishing them in honor of all the beautiful moments you shared before the loss. It's starting that business that you were planning together, building the life that you dreamed about, taking the trip, or enhancing relationships. Even if a job was lost, moving on, would be going into entrepreneurship, or applying to an even better job-not taking no for an answer even if it requires relocating. What was lost can be fuel added to your reasons for doing something better with your life rather than something seen as a betrayal. Let your losses give you a reason to fight harder. Don't waste your tears, your pain has cost you too much.

Those who sow in tears Shall reap in joy.
Psalm 165:5

Pain

Moab had to have felt like a place that reminded her day in and day out of what she had gone through. We can empathize with Naomi in that remaining in a land of famine while going through an emotional famine was not the ideal place. If there was an inkling in her that wanted better, her only option was to leave. We instinctively want to rid ourselves of pain. Therefore, some drink, some smoke, some use sex, and some drown themselves in work, there are many vices. It's all to relieve the pain of the soul.

> Grief is a pain of the soul.

Grief is a pain of the soul. We can say this because we see Naomi's grief speak when she attempts to change her name from Naomi to Mara, which means bitter. After all, she believed God had dealt with her bitterly. She had a "woe is me moment" as she believed God was somehow angry with her and was punishing her. We all know grief can feel like punishment, but this name change was not sanctioned by God. Naomi's pain and sorrow tried to rename her as she attempted to move forward.

Somehow, Naomi, in all of her grief, knew to go where the Lord was. She heard that the Lord was visiting his people. Amid her pain, there was a desire for relief. Though scripture says God was giving the people of Judah food during a famine; the food described is physical food. However, I believe deep down Naomi was after more than physical food. I believe the physical food was a sign to her that God was using to draw her back to Him, to feed her - not just her body but her "soul". Every time a famine had come to an end that had lasted years, joy and praise spread across the land as witnesses of the good news.

The sound of that joy made its way to Naomi somehow. She may have unconsciously moved towards it, but it drew her.

> Your praise adds leverage.

Thankfully, as low as she may have felt, her spirit was in a good enough place to desire to be where the Lord was. We can accurately assess that it was Naomi's soul that needed nourishment just as your soul needs nourishment. Making your way to the residence of the presence of God will be your Judah. Judah means praise. Find your way back to your praise. Even if you must take your pain with you, pick it up, shut it up, and make your way back to moving into His presence. Praise sounds like such an unorthodox thing to do while hurting, it often doesn't make sense and is difficult to move beyond your emotions to do. However, when you make the decision independent of your emotions your spirit will minister to your emotions and begin to provide the remedy for relieving your heaviness. Your praise adds leverage by inviting the

Spirit of the Lord upon you and into your space.

> The garment of praise for the spirit of heaviness.
> Isaiah 61:3

BUT WHY GOD?
David's Men

Sometimes our natural reaction to find and pinpoint a place to lay the pains of our hearts on leads us into a search for "why". Why gives us an answer, a reason, a sense of comfort in answering who or what is responsible for an outcome. But what happens when there is no definite why?

Desperately needing a place to feed our why can dangerously cause harm. Blaming the wrong thing or person will not ease your pain, it will not rid you of the agony of your grief. It only gives you a false sense of control over the emotions that you hide your pain in. You may be angry but that is because you are hurting, my love. Even if there is a pinpointed fault, whether you can validly blame yourself or another will not soothe your soul. At some point, the hunt for blame must end and the truth must be faced. It's gone, they're gone, now what?

> Now it happened, when David and his men came to Ziklag, on the third day, that the Amalekites had invaded the South and Ziklag, attacked Ziklag and burned it with fire, and had taken captive the women and those who were there, from small to great; they did not kill anyone, but carried them away and went their

way. So, David and his men came to the city, and there it was, burned with fire; and their wives, their sons, and their daughters had been taken captive. Then David and the people who were with him lifted up their voices and wept, until they had no more power to weep. And David's two wives, Ahinoam the Jezreelitess, and Abigail the widow of Nabal the Carmelite, had been taken captive. Now David was greatly distressed, for the people spoke of stoning him, because the soul of all the people was grieved, every man for his sons and his daughters. But David strengthened himself in the Lord his God.

I Samuel 30:1-6

David one of the masters of war found himself on the receiving end of the situation he often thrust others into during his battles. He slew tens of thousands as a warrior. Potentially hundreds of thousands of children were left without fathers, wives were left without husbands. Not to mention the times when he and his army of men wiped out entire lineages leaving no successors behind. The tables turned and his men were ambushed by grief while serving his cause as their leader. As you read the story, you'll see all was not lost but for a moment the situation was an epic disaster. They wanted answers to their griefs. Emotions of pain and anger were high as their hearts had been brought low.

When the men lost their wives to the Amalekites their ability to reproduce was taken along with their companionship; when their children were taken their legacy was taken and their names. Burning their city represented the loss of possessions, their harvest was destroyed, and everything they had worked for, was gone. These men were thrust into grief like no other. They were furious, and rightfully so but grief has a way of making anger dangerously unpredictable. As you read David's men gathered amongst themselves, instead of healing and consoling one another they shifted into attack mode towards David their leader. The same David who kept them safe, fed them, and practically provided for them and their families throughout their battles. Their angry grief needed someone to blame because facing the reality of what happened was far too difficult. Lashing out on those who are closest to us is always an easier escape. But it's the wrong one. Many times, when we are hurting the ones closest to us are hurting just as much, though they may not express it in the same way. David's men have taught us to be careful not to attack those who are also in pain with us because we need someone/thing to blame our pain on when we are angry.

In David's men's case, they recovered everything and everyone but let's be honest here, there are things that we will never physically get back, like loved ones who have died, some relationships, or even opportunities. But if we listen a little more closely as we assess the text perhaps the thing to pursue and recover is the joy, security, peace, and reason for living that loss has taken from us.

The way you lose the connection to what is lost is usually the root of your anger. There are so many things attached to different losses: voids that will no longer be filled, the comfortability that the item once afforded you, the sense of accomplishment, and purpose. David and his men temporarily lost their women and children physically but even more than that I believe part of their lamenting was also for what their women and children meant to them. Their love, affection, and reasons for living. Their turning point was when they put down their blame on David who was also hurting and began to pursue what was lost.

Dealing with your anger will be tough but it will also be very necessary. Redirect your anger by facing your pain and examining the real reason you are angry. You must face your anger and other negative emotions because they will prolong your grief if you don't. Being angry, bitter, or frustrated will not make the pain of having to continue life without what was lost any easier. Scream, cry, punch a pillow, go to the gym, take walks, or find a therapist. Do whatever you have to do to let your anger go healthily.

Perhaps in your case, that may mean a moment of reflection on the time spent with a loved one. Were there any goals set between you, trips planned, or ideas of hope for the future that were suddenly halted? When they died seemingly that's what you lost also. When your job ended, maybe the hope of a large purchase or your security in providing did as well. But I say to you get up, prepare yourself to attack grief by pursuing what kept you connected. Arise and complete the mission, you now have a reason to fight harder, go further, and love harder.

David's women and children were collateral damage of war and losing them was painful even if for a moment but the truth that "naked you came into this world and naked you shall leave" remains a matter of fact. I know it's a heavy thing to say and receive but this elephant that takes up too much space must be moved, the heavy must be pushed. Sometimes to move a heavy object takes an even heavier force to do so.

> Grief doesn't discriminate; it chooses leaders too.

Just as David strengthened himself in the Lord you too can be strengthened. Sometimes a leader's pain gets overlooked and they must find an enduring resolve within themselves when they are hurting just as their people are hurting. Because being a leader can tend to be a lonely position that has a stereotype of superhuman strength to a degree, getting tired, hurting, and wanting to quit are not considered to be an option to followers. Depending on how high the regard many followers don't realize they have grown ignorant to the reality that their leader has the challenge of hard times and emotions of grief as well. Consider the business owner who has been in business for years but has come into a low season. He/she is burdened because they have not made enough sales for the past few months and are on the verge of closing but still have to pay their staff and does it with a smile. How about the pastors who have had to lay to rest church member after church member but yet show up on Sunday mornings with a Word of Encouragement? After a while, all that grief weighs on their souls too. Consider the one who is viewed as the strongest of your family who has been laid off and is having problems paying bills, but you have no clue because no one expects the strong to have a moment of what we perceive as weakness. No one checks on the strong, but I encourage you to start. Find a way to inspire those who have been an inspiration to you, you may not know just how much wind you bring to their wings, and before you know it, you'll start to feel the wind under yours. Removing your focus from your grief to relieve someone else's will do you some good. Try it. You'll be surprised.

DARK DAYS

Job

There is a particular narrative of Job's story that I would like for us to unpack as we continue our journey to healing. Job found himself, at one point, overwhelmed by grief. So much so that he lost hope and no longer desired to live.

> Then Job answered and said: "Oh, that my grief were fully weighed, And my calamity laid with it on the scales! For then it would be heavier than the sand of the sea therefore my words have been rash. For the arrows of the Almighty are within me; My spirit drinks in their poison; The

terrors of God are arrayed against me. Does the wild donkey bray when it has grass, or does the ox low over its fodder? Can flavorless food be eaten without salt? Or is there any taste in the white of an egg? My soul refuses to touch them; They are as loathsome food to me. "Oh, that I might have my request, that God would grant me the thing that I long for! That it would please God to crush me, that He would loose His hand and cut me off! Then I would still have comfort; though in anguish I would exult, He will not spare; for I have not concealed the words of the Holy One. "What strength do I have, that I should hope? And what is my end, that I should prolong my life?

Job 6:1-11

I know all too well what it is like to no longer see the benefit of continuing to live and have wanted to die on more than one occasion because of overwhelming hopelessness. At those moments we cannot see forward. Job's story ends very well, with him being restored exponentially. However, he had to get past that moment of grave depression caused by his grief. He could not take his own life. I personally believe Job did not commit suicide because deep down he still knew and believed life was not his to take. The encouraging part of this story was that neither was his life satan's to take.

> Then Job arose, tore his robe, and shaved his head; and fell to the ground and worshiped. And he said: Naked I came from my mother's

womb, and naked shall I return there. The Lord gave, and the Lord has taken away; Blessed be the name of the Lord.

Job 1:21

Your moment may feel unbearable, but you are stronger than you know yourself to be. Grief can tend to make time feel as though it has decided to slow down. But I encourage you to focus only on getting through one hour at a time. There may be times when you feel like you cannot encourage yourself as David did. You may feel more like Job and would rather God let you die because you believe that God has caused your pain. However, if you would read the story of Job, you'll see that God wasn't the one directly responsible for Job's pain.

So satan answered the Lord and said, "Does Job fear God for nothing? Have You not made a hedge around him, around his household, and around all that he has on every side? You have blessed the work of his hands, and his possessions have increased in the land. But now, stretch out Your hand and touch all that he has, and he will surely curse You to Your face!" And the Lord said to Satan, Behold, all that he has is in your power; only do not lay a hand on his person." So satan went out from the presence of the Lord.

Job 1:9-12

Everything that happened to Job were things that satan caused to try to get Job to turn against God. But God refused to remove the protection from His life. Satan literally took everything from Job, his oxen, camels, and donkeys were stolen, all his servants were killed (except three), his sheep were burned, and his children were killed by a tornado all around the same time. Then his friends turned on him, he got sick with painful boils, and his wife spitefully told him to curse God and die. It was as though a domino was struck and tragedy happened one after the other. Have you ever felt like Job? Life got so hard for

Job and his grief was so overwhelming that he hated the day he was born and the day he was conceived.

> May the day perish on which I was born, And the night in which it was said, A male child is conceived. For the thing I greatly feared has come upon me, and what I dreaded has happened to me. I am not as ease, nor am I quiet; I have no rest, for trouble comes.
> Job 3:3,25,26

But even Job's story has a happy ending. If you can just allow those hours to become days, those days will become years. We may have to cry through pain for hours, worship, and write-through grief for days but these moments will teach you how to talk to God throughout your years. Remember, Job had no clue of his story's ending and thought God was taking everything from him instead of satan, but he refused to turn away from God. He did not get angry with God and did not think of God as being wrong.

> **In all this Job did not sin nor charge God with wrong.**
> Job 1:22

I pray you will choose to keep living to find out your ending.

> Weeping may endure for a night, but joy comes in the morning.
>
> Psalms 30:5b

Dark days are an oxymoron, the phrase itself is a contradiction. Days are not intended to be dark, yet sometimes they are because we allow grief to be prolonged. Weeping does not have to endure the entire night and night is not permanent, it's temporary. Please don't allow your grief to be prolonged, don't get stuck there, and Definitely don't end your life in a temporary moment. Morning is coming. The interesting thing about joy coming in the morning is that morning begins in darkness.

Midnight begins the morning, and every midnight is dark, the sun has not risen just yet-day has not begun. But that's when joy comes, it arrives during darkness. Though everything around you may be dark and grim, joy can still come into your dark moment. Joy will strengthen you in ways you never imagined because it is the portal to hope and purpose. It gives you a reason to live. Though you may not feel like it now, you still have a reason to live. When I say live, I mean live in every aspect of the word including allowing yourself to move on and move forward just as our friend Naomi did. Let's make every breathing moment you have left count because it's a sign that your story has more that needs to be narrated.

> Life is not yours to take.

There were moments when Job no longer wanted to live, but thankfully he did not end his own life. Job showed us he believed no matter how hard his life became his life was not his to take. We are not the creators of life therefore we have no right to end a life, God gave us breath, and only He can take it back. Think of it this way, if I gave you a birthday gift your neighbor has no right to come to your house and take it without. Anyone who takes something that does not belong to them is stealing. As believers in Christ, our lives are not our own, our bodies are the temple of Holy Spirit; we have been bought and redeemed by the blood of Christ. Because you have purpose and an expected end of health and prosperity ending one's life during a temporary moment would be robbing yourself of the rewards of completing your process.

In the end, everything that was meant for evil towards Job was used to bring good into his life for four generations.

His turning point was when he repented to God for his thoughts and for saying things concerning God that he did not understand. Job's honest conversation with God changed everything for him. It gave his story an epic ending. You can have the same.

Then Job answered the Lord and said: "I know that You can do everything, and that no purpose of Yours can be withheld from You. You asked, 'Who is this who hides counsel without knowledge?' Therefore, I have uttered what I did not understand, Things too wonderful for me, which I did not know. Listen, please, and let me speak; You said, 'I will question you, and you shall answer Me.' I have heard of You by the hearing of the ear, but now my eye sees You.

Therefore, I abhor myself, and repent in dust and ashes."

Job 42:1-6

> One transparently humble conversation with God can change everything in your life.

For the Lord had accepted Job. And the Lord restored Job's losses when he prayed for his friends. Indeed, the Lord gave Job twice as much as he had before. Then all his brothers, all his sisters, and all those who had been his acquaintances before, came to him and ate food with him in his house; and they consoled him and comforted him for all the adversity that the Lord had brought upon him. Each one gave him a piece of silver and each a ring of gold.

Now the Lord blessed the latter days of Job more than his beginning; for he had fourteen thousand sheep, six thousand camels, one thousand yoke of oxen, and one thousand female donkeys. He also had seven sons and three daughters. And he called the name of the first Jemimah, the name of the second Keziah, and the name of the third Keren-Happuch. In all the land were found no women so beautiful as the daughters of Job; and their father gave them an inheritance among their brothers. After this Job lived one hundred and forty years and saw his children and grandchildren for four generations. So, Job died, old and full of days.

Job 42:9b-17

COLLATERAL DAMAGE

Rizpah

Many of us know the strength of a mother's love. She will be by your side no matter what you go through or what trouble you get yourself into. She doesn't shy away when things get tough, but you can always find a good mother alongside her child fighting. No matter how old you get, great Mothers are support systems of hope, faith, love, and strength. Rizpah is a mother whose love remained undaunted. The powerful part about her story is she teaches us how to love and how to fight for those who cannot fight for themselves - never giving up on those we love. Because Rizpah's story is so rarely told and examined to do it justice I believe it should be read rather than me telling it to you.

There was a famine in David's time. It went on year after year after year—three years. David went to God seeking the reason. God said, "This is because there is blood on Saul and his house, from the time he massacred the Gibeonites." So the king called the Gibeonites together for consultation. (The Gibeonites were not part of Israel; they were what was left of the Amorites, and protected by a treaty with Israel. But Saul, a fanatic for the honor of Israel and Judah, tried to kill them off.) David addressed the Gibeonites: "What can I do for you? How can I compensate you so that you will bless God's legacy of land and people?" The Gibeonites replied, "We don't want any money from Saul and his family. And it's not up to us to put anyone in Israel to death." But David persisted: "What are you saying I should do for you?" Then they told the king, "The man who tried to get rid of us, who schemed to wipe us off the map of Israel—well, let seven of his sons be handed over to us to be executed—hanged before God at Gibeah of Saul, the holy mountain." And David agreed, "I'll hand them over to you." The king spared Mephibosheth, son of Jonathan, the son of Saul, because of the promise David and Jonathan had spoken before God. But the king selected Armoni and Mephibosheth, the two sons that Rizpah daughter of Aiah had borne to Saul, plus the five sons that Saul's daughter Merab had borne to Adriel son of Barzillai the Meholathite. He turned them over to the Gibeonites who hanged them on the mountain before God—all seven died together. Harvest was just getting underway, the beginning of the barley harvest, when they were executed. Rizpah daughter of Aiah took rough burlap and spread it out for herself on a rock from the beginning of the harvest until the heavy rains started. She kept the birds away from the bodies by day and the wild animals by night. David was told what she had done, this Rizpah daughter of Aiah and concubine of Saul. He then went and got the remains of Saul and Jonathan his son from the leaders at Jabesh Gilead (who had rescued them from the town square at Beth Shan where the Philistines had hung them after striking them down at Gilboa). He gathered up their remains and brought them together with the dead bodies of the seven who had just been hanged. The bodies were taken back to the land of Benjamin and given a decent burial in the tomb of Kish, Saul's father. They did everything the king ordered to be done. That cleared things up: from then on God responded to Israel's prayers for the land.

2 Samuel 21:1-14 MSG

> **Collateral damage**
>
> inadvertent casualty among the innocent because of a pledged secondary obligation

Wow, can you imagine what that must have felt like for Rizpah here? Can you relate to her? Rizpah was king Saul's concubine and the daughter of Aiah. Her sons were collateral damage. She's a mother whose sons were hung like pigs that have been slaughtered. They paid the penalty for their father's sin. The offense was not theirs, yet they were sacrificed as payment for a crime they did not commit. That mental image is so familiar for many, and I know it's a tough subject, but there are so many mothers whose sons have been slaughtered in the streets. And as a result, there lie the pains of grief. Some have experienced this through police brutality, some have experienced this through quarrels and gang violence, a lack of opportunities, and some have experienced this through car accidents or drug-related abuses, or overdose.

Nevertheless, sons and daughters have been slaughtered by circumstances of tragic situations and the mothers have been the ones left to ward off vultures who seek to feast on tainting the memories of their young ones. They stand against the slander of their reputation by outsiders and fight stereotypes of the type of lives that their young were living attempting to preserve the truth of who they knew them to be. It's painful to experience and even watch the agony of a mother's grief caused by the sins of generational dysfunction. It's truly an elephant in the room.

Our dearest Rizpah found herself engulfed by unwarranted grief. She was blind- sighted and it hurt. It hurt so much that she couldn't let it go. She couldn't allow her boys to decay exposed and degraded in the streets. Rizpah could not move on nor move forward until she buried them properly, until she laid her pain to rest, until her soul was soothed. She fought the beast of the night and vultures of the day until it got the attention of a king.

There is a type of grief that will cause you to have to weep and fight, night after night until the rain comes. Until you get a response from heaven and the attention of THE KING. You may have to fight for your ability to release what has died because you are physically unable to let it go. After your time of weeping, fighting, and praying a burial will take place. One day a shift will happen, and you'll receive a word from the King, an order to let Him have the remains, and lay your pain rest. Once you release your pain, your soul will rest. But take your moment and weep before God, trust that He will provide relief.

Heavy Lifter

Jesus Christ & Holy Spirit

The Balm of Gilead

Why is Jesus called the Balm of Gilead?

The Bible records that in ancient times there came from Gilead, beyond the Jordan, a substance used to heal and soothe. It came, perhaps, from a tree or shrub, and was a major commodity of trade in the ancient world. It was known as the Balm of Gilead. That name became symbolic of the power to soothe and heal.

Balm

something that has a comforting, soothing, or restorative effect

---

Balm of Gilead was a rare perfume used medicinally that was mentioned in the Hebrew Bible and named after the region of Gilead, where it was produced. The expression stems from William Tyndale's language in the King James Bible of 1611 and has come to signify a universal cure in figurative speech.

The "Balm in Gilead" is a reference from the Old Testament, but the lyric of this spiritual colloquialism refers to the

New Testament concept of salvation through the works and miracles of Jesus Christ. The Balm of Gilead is interpreted as a spiritual medicine that has the ability to heal Israel (and sinners in general). It is a representation encompassing all of whom Christ is to the world: the answer the deliverer, the savior, the healer, the soothing agent, the sweet-smelling savor, and essence of heaven's aroma. Christ is the answer that left us the answer to the grievances of life.

We all know that a person's last words can be words that warrant attention, especially when they know their time on earth is expiring. It is believed that Jesus's last words left us with many clues to the keys to life. Case and point. As Jesus was speaking with His disciples, He began to mentally prepare them for His death. He described it as His departure, they did not know that He was going to be crucified, however, Jesus knew that His time was coming to an end. And because He was such a great and loving leader, He began to reveal deeper insights into the Kingdom. One of which I believe is the greatest answer to life.

And I will pray to the Father, and He shall give you another Comforter, that he may abide with you forever; even the Spirit of truth; who the world cannot receive, because it seeth him not, neither knoweth him: but ye know him; for he dwelleth with you and shall be in you. I will not leave you comfortless: I will come to you.

John 14:16-18KJV

Jesus was letting His disciples know that He knew His death would cause them great grief, sorrow, and even severe lamenting. I encourage you to read the entire book of John with your attention on high alert to the conversations Jesus had with His disciples. Throughout the end of the book of John, Jesus repeatedly says, "look I know it will be tough, but I will send you Comfort".

> But because I have said these things unto you, sorry hath filled your heart. Nevertheless, I tell you the truth; It is expedient for you that I go away: for if I go not away, the Comforter will not come unto you; but if I depart, I will send him unto you.
> John 16:6,7KJV

That Comfort was the Holy Spirit. Jesus's answer to the grief of His twelve disciples that He loved, trained, and spent most of His life and ministry with was the person of the Holy Spirit. The one who is the spirit of truth, He comforts, guides, glorifies, and teaches because He knows all things, and best of all He FILLS. The Holy Spirit is the epitome of the compassion and love that Christ has for us because He didn't just leave us without a way to move on and move forward. He didn't forsake us but gave us a remedy to soothe the pains of our souls. The Holy Spirit, the one who answers the "whys" of our dark days when the weight of the elephant of the collateral damages of life has become overwhelmingly impossible to move.

Fill

to occupy to the extent of capacity

In other words, to fill means to take up an empty space. Now in order for the space to be taken, there must be an act of insertion of sorts and a vessel that can contain that which it is being filled by. The container's design must be compatible with and willing to receive the object that is filling it. I'm attempting to take my time in painting this mental picture. I hope you're still with me. So Jesus, possibly the only one who has proven to love you to death, left you to leave you with something that He knew would be sufficient enough to fill the void that remained after His death. I just have to believe that if Jesus's answer for alleviating His disciple's grief was Holy Spirit, then Holy Spirit is the answer to your grief too! Earlier I said in order for a large object to be moved it would take a greater force or leverage to move it. This elephant of extended grief has taken up too much space in the room of your heart and soul. The Holy Spirit is available and has enough weight and volume to occupy any capacity of grief that you have. He is the Balm in Gilead, the one who was intentionally sent to comfort the hurt, He is the space/void filler.

And finding some disciples he said to them, "Did you receive the Holy Spirit when you believed?" So, they said to him, "We have not so much as heard whether there is a Holy Spirit." And he said to them, "Into what then were you baptized?" So they said, "Into John's baptism." Then Paul said, "John indeed baptized with a baptism of repentance, saying to the people that they should believe on Him who would come after him, that is, on Christ Jesus." When they heard this, they were baptized in the name of the Lord Jesus. And when Paul had laid hands on them, the Holy Spirit came upon them, and they spoke with tongues and prophesied.

Acts 19:2-6

If you then, being evil, know how to give good gifts to your children, how much more will your heavenly Father give the Holy Spirit to those who ask Him!"

Luke 11:13

Do you remember the part of the definition of fill that explained the container must be compatible and willing? Well receiving the Holy Spirit is the same way as you just read, compatibility is your belief in Jesus Christ and accepting salvation and forgiveness of your sins. To be Willing is just to simply desire and ask. Laying on of hands helps but it is not a requirement, this can be only between you and God. Holy Spirit is a gift that God wants you to have because He knows you need Him; Jesus knew it would take more than a belief in who He is to successfully go through the trials and challenges to come. That's why He provided the answer, and that's why every time you cry out to God and it seems like He is ignoring you-it's because He has already provided the answer. The Holy Spirit and His Grace is Sufficient within you.

Earlier during Jesus's ministry, Mary and Martha had an encounter with Jesus that didn't quite feel as pleasant. They may have even felt as though Jesus was ignoring them when they sent for Him. Their brother Lazarus was sick and on the verge of death. When Jesus heard what was going on He waited two days before heading to them. I encourage you to read John 11. While Jesus is on His "delayed" way Lazarus dies and Mary and Martha end up having a funeral for their brother before Jesus arrives. By then, Mary and Martha were so upset because they believed if Jesus would have come when they called Him their brother Lazarus would not have died. Sometimes you may feel as though God is ignoring you or isn't answering no matter how loudly you cry for Him to come to your aid. I ask that you consider maybe there is a reason that you have not discovered yet. There is always a greater purpose, a different angle, or another factor that comes into play. For example, there may be times when someone prays to God for Him to preserve the life of an individual without considering whether that individual has a desire to continue to live. Sometimes we pray and plead with God and make all kinds of deals only to be disappointed when it does not work out like we want it to because we selfishly don't realize that our prayers can never override someone else's will. Nor can it override God's will. That kind of control opens the door for witchcraft prayers. It may feel as though God has ignored you but maybe, just maybe, He was answering the desires of the one whom you were praying for. Please don't misinterpret this truth. There are times when our prayers can bring miracles of healing and restoration; we are supposed to pray. What I'm suggesting is that you reconsider your pain as it relates to your prolonged grief because of things not happening the way you had hoped.

You have not been abandoned, and yes, Jesus does understand and empathize with your pain. Jesus wept too. When Jesus arrived at the grave site of Lazarus, His dear friend, the one He loved, He too felt grief.

So, go ahead and cry, weep, and release. This elephant of grief has been too heavy for you. Let God send you comfort, that is what Holy Spirit is waiting to do. There is grace available for you so that after you have finished crying you can continue on and move forward. It is possible to decide today to make "everyday" count in homage to what was. Don't allow your tears to be wasted but know that there will be some. And when you feel as though you won't heal…remember you can.

> And He said to me, "My grace is sufficient for you, for My strength is made perfect in weakness." Therefore, most gladly I will rather boast in my infirmities, that the power of Christ may rest upon me.
> II Corinthians 12:9

God Bless you, my love,

QuiNina J. Sinceno

(Hug)

5 Stages of grief:

Denial: This can't be happening.

Anger: Why did this happen? Who is to blame?

Bargaining: Make this not happen and I will...

Depression: I can't do this; I don't want to do anything.

Acceptance: I acknowledge that I cannot change what has happened.

Practical FAQs about grief:

- Understand the pain will not go away faster by ignoring it.
- Crying doesn't mean you are weak; not crying doesn't mean you don't feel.
- Grief has no timeframe.

Additional Tools for coping:

- Write a letter for closure or journaling
- Counseling or group therapy
- Exercise to relieve the stress
- Find ways to do something for someone who is in a worse situation than you

Please take a moment to give a Book Review:
quininaj.com/bookreview
Author's Website: quininaj.com
Social media tag: @quininaj

Other Books:

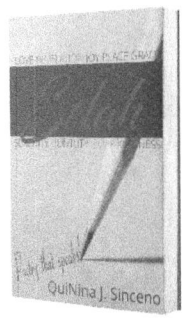